DATE DUE

D1307844

Demco, Inc. 38-293

French AMERICANS

SPIRIT
of America®

French AMERICANS

By Ann Heinrichs

Content Adviser: Adrienne Berney, Ph.D., Curator of Material Culture,
Louisiana State Museum, New Orleans, Louisiana

The Child's World®
Chanhassen, Minnesota

8

*French*AMERICANS

Published in the United States of America by The Child's World®
P.O. Box 326 • Chanhassen, MN 55317-0326 • 800-599-READ • www.childsworld.com

Acknowledgments
The Child's World®: Mary Berendes, Publishing Director

Editorial Directions, Inc.: E. Russell Primm, Editorial Director; Pam Rosenberg, Line Editor; Katie Marsico, Assistant Editor; Matthew Messbarger, Editorial Assistant; Susan Hindman, Copy Editor; Susan Ashley, Proofreader; Julie Zaveloff, Chris Simms, and Peter Garnham, Fact Checkers; Tim Griffin/IndexServ, Indexer; Dawn Friedman, Photo Researcher; Linda S. Koutris, Photo Selector

The Design Lab: Kathleen Petelinsek, Art Direction; Kari Thornborough, Page Production

Photos
Cover/frontispiece: French-Canadian potato farmers in Maine, 1940.

Cover photographs ©: Corbis; Lawrence Manning/Corbis.

Interior photographs ©: AP/Wide World/Andrew J. Cohoon: 28; Bettmann/Corbis: 7, 10, 25; Corbis: 6 (Karen Huntt Mason), 14 (Carl & Ann Purcell), 15 (Wolfgang Kaehler), 19 (Gehl Company), 20 (Michael Busselle), 21 (Philip Gould), 23 (Michael S. Yamashita); Getty Images/Hulton Archive: 8, 9, 12, 13, 17; Magnum Photos/Ian Berry: 22; North Wind Picture Archives: 11, 24 (Nancy Carter), 27.

Registration
The Child's World®, Spirit of America®, and their associated logos are the sole property and registered trademarks of The Child's World®.

Library of Congress Cataloging-in-Publication Data
Heinrichs, Ann.
  French Americans / by Ann Heinrichs.
    v. cm.— (Our cultural heritage)
  Includes index.
  Contents: Exploring the wilderness—Building a new life—French Americans today—Sharing traditions.
  ISBN 1-59296-180-0 (lib. bdg. : alk. paper)
  1. French Americans—Juvenile literature. [1. French Americans.] I. Title. II. Series.
  E184.F8H45 2004
  973'.0441—dc22   2003018095

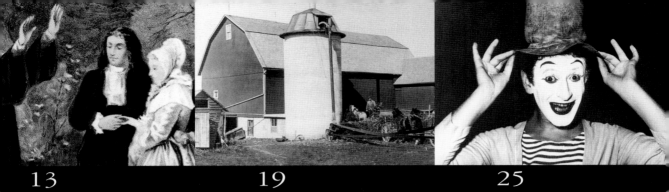

13   19   25

Contents

Chapter ONE

Exploring the Wilderness

DO YOU KNOW ANYONE NAMED NICOLE? HAVE YOU ever eaten a croissant? Did you ever stay in a hotel? All these things have something in common. The

The Fairmont Hotel in San Francisco, California, is one example of how the French language has become an everyday part of American language and culture. This is because "hotel" is a French word.

words *Nicole, croissant,* and *hotel* are all French words that have become a familiar part of the English language.

Much of today's United States once belonged to France. France claimed large amounts of land in North America. French explorers, settlers, and immigrants helped build America from its earliest days.

French people first entered North America in the 1500s. King Francis I of France was interested in the region's fur trade and fishing. He sent explorer Jacques Cartier to present-day Canada. Cartier sailed up into the Saint Lawrence River in 1534. He claimed the river valley for France.

In 1604, French explorers landed on Saint Croix Island off the coast of present-day Maine. It would become part of France's Acadia settlement. In 1608, Samuel de Champlain established the city of Quebec in present-day Canada. It was the first permanent French settlement in North America. This new French **empire** was called New France.

New France grew much bigger in the 1600s. French explorers continued on into the Great Lakes region. From there, they moved south along the

French navigator Jacques Cartier established France's claim to modern-day Canada through his explorations of the Gulf of St. Lawrence and the St. Lawrence River.

Interesting Fact

▸ Many French **missionaries** were also explorers. Father Louis Hennepin explored the Great Lakes region in 1679 and the northern part of the Mississippi River in 1680.

Missionaries wanted to convert the Native Americans to Christianity.

Mississippi River through the heart of today's United States.

Louis Jolliet and Father Jacques Marquette started traveling down the Mississippi River in 1673. They explored the river as far south as present-day Arkansas. René-Robert Cavelier, Sieur de La Salle, went even farther. In 1682, he reached the river's mouth at the Gulf of Mexico. La Salle claimed all the lands in the river **basin** for France. He named this vast region Louisiana, after King Louis XIV of France. New France now covered more than half the North American continent!

Many groups of French people moved into this land. Some were fur traders. They traded with Native Americans for beaver furs. Others were Roman

Catholic missionaries who came to teach their religion to the native people. The French set up forts throughout New France. Hundreds of soldiers were stationed there.

France also sent colonists to settle and farm the land. Merchants and skilled craftspeople joined in, too. The promise of free, fertile land was hard to resist. In the early 1600s, many newcomers settled in Acadia. It included present-day Nova Scotia and part of Maine. Others settled in the Saint Lawrence River Valley.

French trappers and fur traders explored what is now the northern United States and southern Canada. These skilled woodsmen and canoeists were called *voyageurs* (French for "travelers"). They would later be valuable guides for American explorers.

Grand Portage was a highly profitable fur trading post on Lake Superior in 1784. Many French settlers were involved in the fur trade because furs were so highly valued.

THE VOYAGEURS WERE FRENCH-CANADIAN FRONTIERSMEN. THEY EXPLORED THE North American wilderness in the 1700s and early 1800s, traveling mostly by canoe. Their object was to trade with Native Americans for the skins of beavers and other fur-bearing animals. Beaver-fur hats were all the rage in Europe, and their skins could be sold at high prices.

The voyageurs began their trips from Quebec or Montreal. They canoed up the Saint Lawrence River into the Great Lakes. From there, they followed rivers leading north, west, and south. Along the way, they set up fur-trading posts. Many of these posts grew into cities in present-day Canada, Minnesota, and other regions.

Voyageurs made friends with Native Americans and learned many skills from them. They learned to make birch-bark canoes and to survive in the forest. Many of the voyageurs settled in the wilderness and married Native American women. Their children were called the Métis—people of mixed French and Indian blood.

Many French settlements grew up around the Great Lakes. One was Detroit, in present-day Michigan. French fur-trading posts dotted the Great Lakes region, too. Often these posts consisted of only a few log cabins.

The French also made settlements along the Mississippi River. They established Saint Louis, Missouri; Memphis, Tennessee; and Natchez, Mississippi. New Orleans was founded near the mouth of the Mississippi River. It began as a little village with muddy streets. But it would become an important French seaport and trading center.

Many more groups of French people would sail to America's shores. They came because of wars, religious **persecution,** and economic hardships. One and all, they hoped for a better life in America.

In 1701, Antoine Laumet de Lamothe, Sieur de Cadillac, founded the city of Detroit, which he called Pont Chartrain. He built a church and a fort, which attracted more colonists. His goal was to make Detroit "The Paris of the new France."

Interesting Fact

▶ The French pirate Jean Laffite helped General Andrew Jackson win the Battle of New Orleans in the War of 1812 (1812–1815). Laffite was put in charge of the U.S. forces' artillery.

Chapter Two

Building a New Life

SETTLERS IN NEW FRANCE HAD A ROUGH LIFE. THEY chopped down trees, built houses, and planted crops. They hunted animals such as moose, bear, and rabbits for meat. Those who lived in the northern settlements bundled up in fur-lined coats in the cold winters. Their Native American neighbors taught them to wear snowshoes in the snow.

Jean Baptiste Le Moyne was a French explorer, a colonial governor of Louisiana and the founder of New Orleans. He went with his brother Pierre on expeditions to the mouth of the Mississippi River. There they founded a settlement in 1699. Later he commanded the colony of Louisiana and founded New Orleans in 1718. He made New Orleans the colony's capital in 1722.

The Huguenots were one of the many persecuted religious groups that came to America in search of religious freedom. This is a picture of a Huguenot wedding taking place in a forest.

Most early settlers in New France were men. But French officials knew that a colony needed families in order to grow. Hundreds of young women were sent to New France between 1663 and 1673. They were called *filles du roi,* meaning "the king's girls." They were to marry men in New France and start families. That is what they did, and the population grew.

Not long after that, a new wave of French settlers began arriving. They were seeking religious freedom. Roman Catholicism was France's official religion. France, however, had a growing number of Protestants called Huguenots. In 1685, France outlawed the Huguenots' faith. Thousands decided to **emigrate** to America.

13

FRANCE'S ACADIA COLONY WAS FAR AWAY FROM THE LARGER SETTLEMENT OF Quebec. Acadia lay on the Atlantic coast. Its capital city of Port Royal was in present-day Nova Scotia.

Isolated from other settlers, the Acadians developed their own ways of life. Many tasks were shared by the whole community. When a couple got married, villagers cleared the land and built them a house. It was a fun event, with plenty of food and fiddle music.

Acadian farmers grew wheat, rye, beans, and many other crops. They raised chickens, sheep, and hogs brought from France. The Acadians lived in peace with their Native American neighbors, the Micmac, and traded with them for furs. Acadians had trade ties with the New England colonies, too. From New England came cooking pots, axes, gunpowder, and fabric. In return, the Acadians provided grain, cattle, and furs.

Many Acadian men were fishermen. Their wives and daughters knitted nets for fishing boats and lobster traps. Other Acadians were shipbuilders. The houses they built were as sturdy as their ships. Men chopped down trees and shaped the trunks into squared logs. They fit the logs together to build their homes. They filled any gaps between logs with **caulk,** as they did with ships.

Poor farmers and fishermen lived simple lives. Their homes had dirt floors and a stone fireplace for cooking and heat. People slept on mattresses stuffed with straw. Wealthier merchants and lumbermen could afford better homes. They had wood-plank floors, iron stoves, and proper beds.

The Huguenots settled in New York, Pennsylvania, South Carolina, and other British-American colonies. They hoped to find religious tolerance in those colonies, where most of the British settlers were members of Protestant faiths. These immigrants proved to be skilled workers in many trades and crafts. They blended in with their neighbors, and many changed their French names to English.

Meanwhile, France and Great Britain fought to control North American lands. Great Britain's American colonies lined the Atlantic coast. As colonists pushed westward, they clashed with French settlements. In some cases, both Britain and France claimed the same areas.

In 1755, the British began throwing French settlers out of Acadia. This was called *Le Grand Dérangement* ("The Great Disturbance"). Thousands of Acadians were driven from their homes. British soldiers burned their houses and barns. They herded the Acadians onto ships and sent them back to France.

Some Acadians simply scattered throughout the American colonies. Others moved south of the Saint Lawrence River. They made new homes in present-day Maine, Vermont, and other parts of New England. Hundreds of Acadians settled in southern Louisiana. They came to be called *Cajuns*—a form of the word *Acadians.* Years later, many Acadians who had been forced to return to

France would travel to Louisiana and join those who had already settled there.

Some of the French who settled in Louisiana were businesspeople. They profited from the booming trade in the port of New Orleans. Others were farmers who raised tobacco, rice, and **indigo.**

In 1763, Britain won all of New France east of the Mississippi River, except for New Orleans. French Canadians suddenly found themselves under British rule. At the same time, the American colonists wanted to be free of Britain. Now France and the colonists had a common enemy—Great Britain. France would soon play a big role in the struggle for American independence.

The colonists fought for their freedom in the American Revolutionary War (1775–1783). They quickly realized they needed help to beat the British. Naturally, France came to mind. As early as 1777, a wealthy French merchant was secretly sending guns, ammunition, and money to the colonists. In 1778, the French formed a treaty of alliance with the colonies. They sent thousands of soldiers and seamen to help. The Marquis de Lafayette,

The Marquis de Lafayette was a great help to the colonists during the Revolutionary War. In 1777, he bought a ship, found a crew of men ready for battle, and set sail for America to fight in the revolution against the British. Lafayette was assigned to George Washington's army and he led American forces to many victories.

a French soldier, offered his services for no pay. He led the colonists to many victories.

In 1781, Lafayette led a colonial army against the British in Yorktown, Virginia. There the British were forced to surrender. This was the last great victory of the Revolutionary War. The new United States hailed Lafayette as a hero.

In 1803, France sold its lands west of the Mississippi River to the United States. This is called the Louisiana Purchase. Meriwether Lewis and William Clark explored these western lands from 1804 to 1806. Many of the men who joined their expedition were French-Canadian voyageurs, or sons of voyageur fathers and Native American mothers. They were expert woodsmen who knew the region well.

Events in France would send more immigrants to America. French farmers suffered many crop failures in the 1840s. Also, working-class people had miserable lives and few rights. Poverty and war pushed some people to seek a better life in the United States. In 1851, more than 20,000 people left France for the United States. Some settled in big cities such as New York City. Others made homes in the Midwest or California.

The next wave of French-speaking immigrants came from Canada. They began arriving in the late 1800s. Many came from the province of Quebec. Farmers there struggled with poor soil and not enough farmland. Lumber workers and factory workers suffered low wages and poor living conditions.

At the same time, New England's economy was booming. Hundreds of water-powered factories and mills had grown up along the rivers. Thousands of French Canadians poured in to work in textile mills, paper mills, and shoe factories. Many worked 12 hours a day or more. They formed communities with French-speaking churches, schools, and shops. They were called the Québecois, or people of Quebec.

Other French Canadians found work in Michigan, Illinois, Wisconsin, and Minnesota. In time, they took on the lifestyles of their American neighbors. Still, they cherished the memory of their ancestors and never forgot the hardships that brought them to America.

Many French Canadians found work on farms in the Midwest, such as this farm in Wisconsin.

Chapter THREE

French Americans Today

The French Quarter of New Orleans is an area known all over the world as one of the most vibrant and historically important places in the United States.

MORE THAN 12 MILLION AMERICANS CLAIM FRENCH or French-Canadian **ancestry.** In most places, French-Americans don't stand out as a distinct group. Their ancestors adjusted to American life and mixed in with its culture. Louisiana, however, kept a strong French flavor.

THE FIRST ACADIANS ARRIVED IN LOUISIANA IN 1764. THEY WERE HUNGRY and scared. Their surroundings were unfamiliar, too. They had left a cool climate for the hot, steamy **bayous** of southern Louisiana. There the rivers bend and twist through swampy land, and Spanish moss drapes down from the trees.

Over time, other Louisianians mispronounced *Acadians* and called these people Cajuns. The Cajuns lived by farming, fishing, and trapping. Men hollowed out cypress logs to make canoes called pirogues. These boats glided smoothly through the rivers and swamps. Women carried on their traditions, too. They used spinning wheels to make yarn and looms to weave the yarn into clothes and blankets.

Cajuns developed a cooking style based on local ingredients. This style was also influenced by nearby groups such as the Creoles and Native Americans. They made dozens of dishes with shrimp and crawfish. Cajuns developed their own music style, too. A fiddle, accordion, and triangle provide the music for their songs and dances.

Today, many Cajuns still live by farming and fishing. They raise rice, sugarcane, corn, sweet potatoes, and okra. Cajun fishers catch oysters, shrimp, crawfish, and crabs. Other Cajuns hold jobs in their communities. For example, many Cajuns are skilled workers in Louisiana's oil and gas industry.

In Louisiana, almost one out of five people have French or Cajun ancestors. They may have last names such as Landry, Hébert, or Thibodeaux. Many southern Louisiana cities have a French flavor. That's especially true in New Orleans, the largest city.

Cajuns still live in southern Louisiana. They speak a distinct Cajun dialect. It's based on the French language of their Acadian ancestors. Mixed in are words and phrases from English, Spanish, Native American, and African-American people.

Lafayette is known as Louisiana's Cajun capital. The city honors its culture in many ways. One is Vermilionville, a living-history museum. "Acadians" in costume share traditional stories, music, and cooking. Vermilionville also tells the story of the Creoles—French-speaking people who are of mixed

Taking a trip to Lafayette's Vermilionville is like taking a time machine into the past. Vermilionville occupies 23 acres (9.3 hectares) of land, recreating an Acadian village from the years 1765 to 1890. This simple bedroom in a wooden house at Vermilionville helps teach visitors how the Acadians lived.

European (Spanish or French) and African-American heritage. Lafayette's Acadian Village is an outdoor museum. It preserves Acadian homes, a general store, and a blacksmith shop. Lafayette also celebrates the *Festivals Acadiens* every year.

In New England, French culture is very much alive in Maine. French Americans are the largest ethnic group in that state. Tens of thousands of people in Maine speak French every day. Most live along the Saint John River, next to the Canadian border. Others live around Lewiston or Biddeford. They are the descendants of French-Canadian mill workers.

Lewiston's Little Canada neighborhood was once bustling with French bakeries and food markets. But once the mills closed, the community declined. Lewiston still celebrates its French **heritage** with the *Festival de Joie,* or Festival of Joy.

The St. John River Valley forms part of the international border between Canada and the United States. The valley is unique because its people have tried to hold on to their traditions and customs as French Americans.

Interesting Fact

▶ Almost one-fourth of the people in Maine have French ancestors. Vermont, Rhode Island, and New Hampshire have an even higher share of French Americans. More than one-fourth of their residents claim a French heritage.

23

People can try their hand at French crafts or even join in a **crêpe**-eating contest!

Biddeford holds a French festival called *La Kermesse*. Madawaska, in the Saint John Valley, holds the Acadian Festival. Actors at the festival recreate the Acadians' first landing in northern Maine. The Franco-American Women's Institute is based in Brewer, Maine. It preserves women's traditional arts and crafts. That includes knitting, quilting, baking, and jam making.

Vermont, Rhode Island, and New Hampshire are home to many French Americans, too. Manchester, New Hampshire's largest city, attracted thousands of French Canadians. Its Amoskeag mills were once the world's largest textile producers. French-Canadian mill workers lived in the Little Canada community, on the west side of town.

Massachusetts is a rather small state. However, it has one of the highest French-American populations in the country. French Canadians settled in Lowell, Worcester, and other mill towns.

French people also have a long history in California. The city of Santa Barbara holds the largest

The rapid expansion of cotton manufacturing in the 18th century was an important part of the Industrial Revolution. With modern inventions such as these power looms, products could be mass-produced instead of handmade.

Marcel Marceau is considered the world's greatest mime. He was born in Strasbourg, France. Many French-American festivals feature this silent art form that is often associated with their home country.

French festival in the western United States. It's the *Fête Française,* or French Festival. It takes place around July 14. That's Bastille Day, which celebrates the French Revolution of 1789. It features music, wandering **mimes** and jugglers, puppet plays, and French food.

As you see, some French people have held on to their traditions. Others joined in with their neighbors to become simply "Americans." Still, these descendants are proud of the French heritage that makes them special.

Interesting Fact

▸ The Bastille was a French prison that became a symbol of what the French people disliked about being ruled by a king. Bastille Day marks the anniversary of the storming of the Bastille by the people of France on July 14, 1789. After this historic event, he king realized he could no longer hold on to his power and France became a republic, a country governed by officials elected by the people.

Sharing Traditions

▶ In 1986, the Statue of Liberty was 100 years old. It had massive repairs before its anniversary. A team of French workers came over to help rebuild the statue. They used many of the same techniques the original builders had used.

LOOK AT THE STATUE OF LIBERTY. MORE THAN ANY other symbol, it stands for America and its freedoms. The statue is also a symbol of friendship between France and America. It was a gift from the French people. They were proud to have helped Americans gain independence. America also inspired the French to fight for their freedom in 1789.

So in 1876, when it was the 100th anniversary of the Declaration of Independence, the French people wanted to celebrate. They built the Statue of Liberty as a birthday gift to the United States. In 1886, it was unveiled on an island in New York Harbor.

The nation's capital of Washington, D.C., has a French connection, too. It was designed by the French-American architect Pierre Charles L'Enfant. Its streets, parks, buildings, and monuments are beautiful. They are also laid out in a very orderly way. This layout represents American ideals of equality and justice.

Dozens of American cities today have French names. These names were given by French traders or settlers hundreds of years ago. A French explorer founded Detroit, Michigan, in 1701. Its name is French for "strait" or "channel." Much later, a car was named after Detroit's founder—Antoine Laumet de Lamothe, Sieur de Cadillac.

Vincennes, Indiana, began as a French fort in 1732. It was named after a French army officer. Des Moines, Iowa; Des Plaines, Illinois; and La Crosse, Wisconsin, are some other French city names. After the American Revolution, people were grateful to the Marquis de Lafayette. They named many streets, cities, and counties after him.

Do you know anyone named Adrian, Antoine, Colette, or Monique? These are all French names. Hundreds of everyday words have come from the French language. *Restaurant* and *chandelier* are just two examples.

Even in colonial times, French fashions were popular. They featured lace, ribbons, hoop skirts, fancy shoes, and powdered wigs. These styles spread from Paris, France, to London, England. From there, they caught on in America. French clothing designs are still popular in the United States. Their labels may bear the names of designers such as Chanel, Yves Saint Laurent, Pierre Cardin, or Christian Dior.

The French have always been leaders in fashion and style. France has long been known as a place to find the latest and greatest styles around, such as these fashions from the 1770s. We even use the French term haute couture *which means "high fashion" when we speak about the latest fashion trends.*

Lots of foods we enjoy are "immigrants" from France. They include croissants, quiche, omelettes, mousse, crêpes, éclairs, and soufflés. Louisiana hot sauce and blackened fish are some Cajun treats.

French immigrants brought their Mardi Gras festival to America. Many cities with French-American residents celebrate this springtime carnival. But New Orleans's Mardi Gras is the most spectacular of all. More than a million people jam the streets every year. They wear colorful costumes, watch fantastic parades, and dance to the music.

Clearly, French culture is very much a part of America. French people were here long before there even was a United States. It wasn't always easy for French immigrants to make new homes in America. Yet they shared their talents and traditions to make life richer for us all.

The Rex Organization float in the annual Mardi Gras parade in New Orleans is one example of the colorful and creative culture of French Americans.

1534   The French explorer Jacques Cartier claims the Saint Lawrence River Valley for France.

1604   French explorers land on Saint Croix Island, off the coast of Maine.

1608   Samuel de Champlain establishes the Quebec settlement.

1673   Louis Jolliet and Father Jacques Marquette explore the Mississippi River.

1682   René-Robert Cavelier, Sieur de La Salle, claims the Mississippi River basin for France and names it Louisiana.

1685   Huguenots face persecution in France; many emigrate to America.

1718   The city of New Orleans in founded.

1755   British soldiers begin expelling French settlers from Acadia; many Acadians settle in Louisiana and New England.

1763   Great Britain takes over all of New France east of the Mississippi River except for New Orleans.

1781   The Marquis de Lafayette leads the colonists to defeat British forces in Yorktown, Virginia; this is the last great victory of the Revolutionary War.

1789   The French Revolution begins, leading to France's independence.

1803   In the Louisiana Purchase, the United States buys France's Louisiana territory; this more than doubles the size of the United States.

1804–1806   Meriwether Lewis and William Clark explore the Louisiana territory; they use French-Canadian voyageurs as guides.

1848   A revolution in France leads many French people to leave for America.

2004   French Americans celebrate 400 years of French history in America.

ancestry (AN-sess-tree)
A family's ancestry is its original nation or race. Millions of people of French ancestry live in the United States.

basin (BAY-suhn)
A river's basin is the area whose waters eventually flow into that river. La Salle claimed the Mississippi River's basin for France in 1682.

bayous (BYE-ooz)
Bayous are slow-moving bodies of water going through a swamp. They flow into or out of a lake or river. Acadians settled in the bayou region of Louisiana.

caulk (KAWK)
Caulk is a waterproof material used to seal cracks in ships and buildings. Acadians used caulk in building ships and log cabins.

crêpe (KRAPE)
A crêpe is a thin pancake that's often rolled up with a sweet filling inside. The French serve crêpes as a dessert.

emigrate (EM-uh-grate)
To emigrate is to leave one's home country to make a home in another country. Thousands of Huguenots emigrated from France to America in the 1600s.

empire (EM-pire)
An empire is a large group of countries or territories under one ruler. France built a huge empire in North America in the 1600s.

heritage (HEHR-uh-tij)
A person's heritage consists of traditions passed down from parent to child over a long period of time. French language, foods, and festivals are all part of French Americans' heritage.

indigo (IN-duh-goh)
Indigo is a plant that is used to make a dark purple-blue dye. In the 18th century, French farmers in Louisiana raised tobacco, rice, and indigo.

mimes (MIMES)
Mimes are performers who tell a story without speaking, using only body movements. Today in France, mimes perform both on the stage and in the streets.

missionaries (MISH-uh-ner-eez)
Missionaries are people sent by their church, often to foreign countries, to spread their religion. Jacques Marquette and Louis Hennepin were Roman Catholic missionaries who were also explorers.

persecution (purr-suh-KYOO-shuhn)
Persecution is mistreatment of those who have different beliefs. Huguenots suffered persecution in Roman Catholic France because of their Protestant beliefs.

Web Sites

Visit our homepage for lots of links about French Americans:
http://www.childsworld.com/links.html

Note to Parents, Teachers, and Librarians:
We routinely verify our Web links to make sure they're safe,
active sites—so encourage your readers to check them out!

Books

Parent, Michael, and Julien Olivier (translators). *Of Kings and Fools: Stories of the French Tradition in North America.* Little Rock, Ark.: August House, 1996.

Stone, Amy. *French Americans.* New York: Marshall Cavendish, 1995.

Tallant, Robert, and Corinne Boyd Dillon (illustrator). *Evangeline and the Acadians.* Gretna, La.: Pelican, 2000.

Places to Visit or Contact

Acadian Village
To see buildings that illustrate what life was like for the Acadians in Maine in the 1700s and 1800s
U.S. Route 1
Van Buren, ME
207/868-5042

Voyageurs National Park
To see some of the oldest exposed rock formations in the world, as well as the land and waters explored by the voyageurs
3131 Highway 53
International Falls, MN 56649
218/283-9821

Index

About the Author

ANN HEINRICHS GREW UP IN FORT SMITH, ARKANSAS, AND LIVES IN Chicago, Illinois. She is the author of more than 100 books for children and young adults on Asian, African, and U.S. history and culture. After many years as a children's book editor, she enjoyed a successful career as an advertising copywriter. She has also written numerous newspaper, magazine, and encyclopedia articles.

32